Cheetahs like open spaces where they can run fast

Cheetahs are big, wild cats. They are the fastest land animals in the world. There are three kinds of cheetahs. Most cheetahs live on the **continent** of Africa. A few live outside of Africa in the country of Iran.

continent one of Earth's seven big pieces of land

CHEETAHS

BY KATE RIGGS

CREATIVE EDUCATION

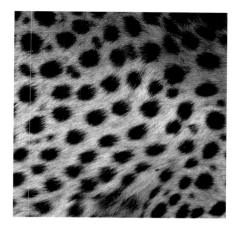

Cheetahs have bodies covered with spotted fur. Their fur looks like a leopard's fur. But each cheetah's spots are different. A cheetah has black lines of fur on the sides of its nose. These marks are called tear lines.

A cheetah has spots everywhere except on its throat and belly

A male cheetah weighs about 140 pounds (64 kg). Females weigh about 90 pounds (41 kg). A cheetah grows until its body is about four feet (1.2 m) long. Its tail is about 30 inches (76 cm) long.

Cheetahs are much smaller cats than lions and tigers

*A cheetah may walk a long
way while hunting for food*

Most cheetahs live on the African savannas. A cheetah's spotted and tan-colored fur helps it hide in the tall grasses. Some cheetahs live in hot, dry lands called deserts.

savannas flat, hot lands covered with grass and a few trees

Cheetahs eat meat.

Some of their favorite animals to eat are antelopes (*AN-teh-lopes*) and gazelles (*gah-ZELZ*). Sometimes cheetahs eat rabbit-like animals called hares, too.

Gazelles are fast runners, but cheetahs are even faster

*Cheetah cubs have fluffy
fur that is partly gray*

A mother cheetah has two to five **cubs** at a time. At first, the mother moves her cubs from place to place. She does this to keep them safe from **predators**. Hyenas and lions sometimes kill cheetah cubs. When the cubs are seven months old, they learn how to hunt. Wild cheetahs can live for 7 to 12 years.

cubs baby cheetahs

predators ar   that kill and eat other animals

Some cheetahs live alone. But most cheetahs live and hunt in groups. Many male cheetahs hunt together in groups called coalitions (*coh-ah-LIH-shunz*).

Cheetahs in coalitions stay together their whole lives

A running cheetah can go
100 feet (30 m) in 1 second

Cheetahs hunt in the morning or late in the day. They do not like to hunt when it is very hot. Cheetahs run fast to catch their prey. They can run up to 70 miles (121 km) per hour! But sometimes they are not fast enough.

prey animals that are eaten by other animals

Today, some people go to Africa to see cheetahs in the wild. Other people visit zoos to see cheetahs. It is exciting to see these fast cats up-close!

A cheetah may jump up in a tree to look around for prey

A Cheetah Story

Why do cheetahs have tear lines? People in Africa used to tell a story about this. They said that there was once a lazy hunter. One day, he stole three cheetah cubs when the mother left to hunt. He wanted the cheetahs to do his hunting for him. The mother cheetah cried because she could not find her cubs. The tears made black marks on the sides of her nose. From then on, all cheetahs have had tear lines!

Read More

Eckart, Edana. *Cheetah*. New York: Children's Press, 2005.

Hansen, Rosanna. *Caring for Cheetahs*. Honesdale, Penn.: Boyds Mills Press, 2007.

Web Sites

Enchanted Learning: Cheetahs
http://www.enchantedlearning.com/subjects/mammals/cheetah/coloring.shtml
This site has cheetah facts and a picture to color.

National Geographic Kids Creature Feature: Cheetahs
http://kids.nationalgeographic.com/Animals/CreatureFeature/Cheetah
This site has pictures and videos of cheetahs.

Index